Welcome to Saudi Arabia

By Bob Temple

The
**Child's
World**®

Published by The Child's World®
1980 Lookout Drive
Mankato, MN 56003-1705
800-599-READ
www.childsworld.com

Content Adviser: Professor Paul Sprachman, Vice Director, Center for Middle
Eastern Studies, Rutgers, The State University of New Jersey, New Brunswick, NJ
Design and Production: The Creative Spark, San Juan, Capistrano, CA
Editorial: Emily J. Dolbear, Brookline, MA
Photo Research: Deborah Goodsite, Califon, NJ

Cover and title page photo: Mehmet Biber/Photri
Interior photos: Alamy: 3 middle, 8 (vario images GmbH & Co.KG), 3 top, 19 (Robert
Harding Picture Library Ltd), 20 (Kevpix), 23 (Trip), 25 (LOOK Die Bildagentur der
Fotografen GmbH); AP Photo: 13 (Amr Nabil), 17 (David Longstreath), 30 (Hasan
Jamali); Art Resource: 11 (Giraudon); Getty Images: 9 (Reza), 14 (Hassan Ammar/
AFP), 24 (Wayne Eastep/Stone); iStockphoto.com: 18 (atbaei), 28 (Ufuk Zivana), 29
(dirkr), 31 (rotofrank); Landov: 21 (Zainal Abd Halim/Reuters), 22, 27 (Sultan al
Fahed/Reuters); Lonely Planet Images: 3 bottom, 16 (Anthony Ham); NASA Earth
Observatory: 4 (Reto Stockli); Panos Pictures: 7 (Andrew Testa); Peter Arnold, Inc.: 10,
15 (Das Fotoarchiv.); Photo Researchers, Inc.: 6 (Ray Ellis).
Map: XNR Productions: 5

Library of Congress Cataloging-in-Publication Data
Temple, Bob.
  Welcome to Saudi Arabia / by Bob Temple.
      p. cm. — (Welcome to the world)
  Includes index.
  ISBN 978-1-59296-975-3 (library bound : alk. paper)
  1. Saudi Arabia—Juvenile literature. I. Title. II. Series.

  DS204.25.T365 2008
  953.8—dc22
                                            2007036351

Contents

Where Is Saudi Arabia?

On the other side of the world, a group of countries make up an area called the Middle East. The Middle East is located in the southwestern part of the **continent** of Asia. That's near where Asia meets with the continent of Africa.

Saudi Arabia is surrounded by seven different countries. It is also surrounded on two sides by bodies of water—the Persian Gulf and the Red Sea.

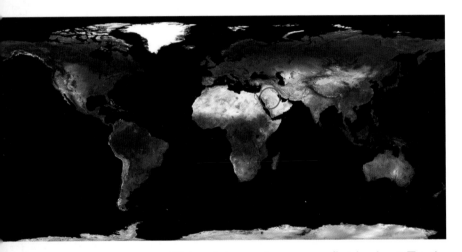

This picture gives us a flat look at Earth. Saudi Arabia is inside the red circle.

Did you **know?**

Saudi Arabia is the largest country in the Middle East.

4

The Land

Saudi Arabia is very hot and dry. Much of the country is made up of dry, sandy deserts. Here temperatures can reach as high as 130 degrees Fahrenheit (54 degrees Celsius)! The central part of the country gets no more than about 4 inches (10 centimeters) of rain a year, so only small plants can grow there.

The Rub al-Khali is one of the largest sand deserts in the world.

A Saudi boy and his grandfather wade into the Red Sea at dusk.

On the western side of the country, along the Red Sea, is flat, often treeless land called a **plain.** This area receives more rainfall.

The eastern side of the country, along the Persian Gulf, contains underground oil fields. This oil provides Saudi Arabia's main business. In the southernmost part of Saudi Arabia is a large desert called the Rub al-Khali, or "Empty Quarter."

Plants and Animals

All plants and animals need water to survive. Some need less water than others. Because Saudi Arabia gets so little rainfall, only certain kinds of plants and animals can live there. The

land along the Red Sea contains more plants than the rest of the country. But those plants are mostly herbs and shrubs.

Even without much rain, Saudi Arabia has many types of animals. Highland areas have mountain goats, wildcats, baboons, wolves, hyenas, and foxes. There are also gazelles and camels. Birds that live in Saudi Arabia include eagles, falcons, and hawks.

A Saudi baboon looks at the sunset.

Did you know?

An **oasis** (left) is a place in the desert where plants can grow. An oasis gets its water from underground springs.

During daily prayer, all Muslims must face toward a stone building in Mecca called the *Kaaba.*

Long Ago

Thousands of years ago, groups of **nomads** lived on the land that is now called Saudi Arabia. Nomads are people who do not stay in one place all year but move around as the seasons change. They live off the plants and animals around them. In

Saudi Arabia, many nomads have herds of camels, goats, and sheep.

Over time, people began to settle in different parts of the country. Communities began to grow. In the early 600s, the Saudi city of Mecca was the birthplace of the religion called **Islam.**

As years passed, different groups struggled over what is now Saudi Arabia. Then in 1902, a leader named Ibn Saud took control of the area. He made himself the ruler of a new kingdom of Saudi Arabia in 1932. Soon after, underground oil was discovered. Because the world needs oil, Saudi Arabia became a very important country.

Did you know?

Muhammad was the founder of the religion called Islam. Born in about 570, he preached in Mecca (left) and Medina. They became Islam's most important cities. Muhammad died in 632.

Saudi Arabia Today

Many different people have ruled Saudi Arabia since 1902. There has been lots of fighting for control of the land and its oil. The fighting limited the country's progress in many ways.

Crown Prince Faisal became king in 1964. Many things improved during his rule. More people were allowed to get an education. People were given more freedom to choose things such as what kind of music to listen to.

In 1982, King Fahd became the ruler of the country. He made the Saudi government more modern in 1992. Saudi Arabia is still a **monarchy,** which means the king has power over the people. Crown Prince Abdullah took over in 2005.

Saudi Arabia has been friendly with the United States. In 1991, U.S. troops were allowed to set up operations in Saudi Arabia during the **Gulf War.** The United States helped defend Saudi Arabia against attacks from Iraq. In 2003, Saudi Arabia quietly supported the war with Iraq.

King Abdullah speaks at a meeting of the League of Arab States in 2007. The organization's seal is behind him.

The People

Most Saudis are Arabs. They are related to the people who lived on the same land thousands of years before. The Saudi people are also **Muslims.** The Saudis follow many religious rules. For example, women in public must wear black cloaks that cover their bodies from head to toe.

Women cross a street in Mecca. In Saudi Arabia's cities, some women don't cover their face.

Muslim men in Saudi Arabia kneel to pray.

The Holy Book of Islam is called the Koran. It says that all Muslims, if they have enough money, must visit Mecca. About two million Muslims visit Mecca every year to pray at the Great Mosque. A mosque is the building where Muslims pray.

15

The Kingdom Tower and
city skyline of Riyadh

City Life and Country Life

A Bedouin boy washes his face at a camel market in Hofuf.

Many people in Saudi Arabia live in or near large cities. These cities are usually very crowded. They have both old and new places to live, including very tall apartment buildings.

Some Saudi people live away from the city. Some live in the few areas of Saudi Arabia where crops and animals can survive. Other Saudis, called Bedouins, or "original people," are nomads. Bedouins move around, but they spend a lot of time living in the desert. They travel on camels and drink camel's milk to survive while they cross the desert.

A Saudi road sign in both Arabic and English

Schools and Language

For a long time, girls in Saudi Arabia were not allowed to attend school. That has changed. Now, all children have a chance to go to school—but many do not. More than one-fifth of Saudi Arabia's people cannot read or write.

All Saudis speak Arabic, but they speak different forms or **dialects** of the language. That means that Arabic in one area of the country might sound different from Arabic in other areas. Many Saudis also speak English for business reasons.

Did you know?

More than 200 million people speak Arabic as their first language.

These Saudi schoolboys live in the northeast part of the country.

A Saudi builder works on a construction site in Jidda.

Work

Oil is the most important industry in Saudi Arabia. Much of the world gets its oil from Saudi Arabia's huge underground supply. Oil companies from other

Bank workers in Riyadh check the stock markets on their computers.

countries, including the United States, pay the Saudi government for its oil. The oil industry hires many Saudis to drill for, clean, and ship oil around the world.

Another important industry is construction. Many Saudis work constructing buildings, roads, and more. Others mine for gold, silver, lead, and copper. Some make crafts such as weaving and embroidery. Others fish for a living. Because of a lack of rainfall, only a few Saudis work in farming.

Food

The Saudi people usually have their biggest meal in the middle of the afternoon. At this time they have meat such as beef, chicken, or lamb. They also eat rice, vegetables, fruit, pita bread, and salad. Saudis love to drink rich coffee. Some people have it at every meal.

At other meals, Saudis also enjoy eggs, cheese, beans, and soup. Much of the food Saudis eat comes from other countries.

A Saudi man pours a cup of Arabian coffee.

Many Saudis shop for spices and other foods at open-air markets.

This camel race outside of Riyadh takes place every year.

Pastimes

One of the oldest pastimes in Saudi Arabia is camel racing. Camels in these races can go as fast as 25 miles (40 kilometers) per hour! Saudis also like horse racing.

In recent years, sports from other nations have become popular. Soccer and

A Saudi boy practices soccer at his school playground.

basketball are especially popular. Many Saudis enjoy gymnastics, swimming, and track and field. Watching television programs from around the world is also a common pastime.

Holidays

Saudi Arabia has two main religious holidays. The first is Eid ul-Adha, or "Feast of the Sacrifice." This joyful celebration can last several days. The other is Eid ul-Fitr, or "Feast of the Breaking of the Fast." It comes at the end of the month of Ramadan. During Ramadan, Muslims go without eating, or fast, from sunrise to sunset.

Saudis also celebrate on September 23. This is the day Saudi Arabia became a country under that name.

Saudi Arabia is a fascinating country with a long history. If you ever visit Saudi Arabia, you will find lots of interesting things to see and do!

These Saudis pray to mark the end of Ramadan.

Area: 830,000 square miles (2,149,690 square kilometers)—slightly more than one-fifth the size of the United States

Population: About 27 million people

Capital City: Riyadh

Other Important Cities: Jidda, Mecca, Medina, Ad-Dammam, Dhahran, and Hofuf

Money: The Saudi riyal

National Language: Arabic

National Holiday: Unification Day on September 23 (1932)

National Flag: A green flag with a white sword and white Arabic writing. In English, the words mean "There is no God but Allah and Muhammad is His Prophet."

Head of State and Government: The king of Saudi Arabia

Famous People:

Sami Al-Jaber: athlete

Rajaa Al-Sanea: novelist

Faisal: king of Saudi Arabia from 1964 to 1975

Ibn Saud: founder of modern-day Saudi Arabia, king of Saudi Arabia from 1932 to 1953

Khalid: king of Saudi Arabia from 1975 to 1982

Talal Maddah: musician

Muhammad: founder of Islam

Abdelrahman Munif: novelist

Nimah Nawwab: poet

National Song: "Long Live the King" (or *"Aash Al Maleek"*). It became Saudi Arabia's national song in 1950.

Hasten to glory and supremacy!
Glorify the Creator of the heavens
And raise the green, fluttering flag,
Carrying the emblem of Light!
Repeat—God is greatest!

O my country,
My country, may you always live,
The glory of all Muslims!
Long live the King,
For the flag and the country!

Saudi Recipe*: **Mint Tea**

This recipe is for a tasty hot mint drink.

3 cups boiling water
3 tablespoons dried mint or ½ cup fresh mint
1 pinch ground saffron
sugar

Boil the water in a kettle. Wash the mint and put it in a saucepan. Add the saffron, sugar, and boiling water to saucepan and stir. Bring almost to a boil. Carefully remove saucepan from heat, pour into cups, and serve.

Always ask an adult for permission and help when using the kitchen.

 **How** Do You Say...

ENGLISH	HOW TO SAY IT IN ARABIC
hello	ahl sah-LAHM ah-ah-LAY-koom
good-bye	mah ah-e-sah-LEH-mah
please	min FOD-lak *(to a man)* min FOD-lik *(to a woman)*
thank you	SHO-krahn
one	WAH-hed
two	ith-NEEN
three	tah-LEH-tha
yes	NAAM
no	LEH

30

Glossary

continent (KON-tih-nent) A continent is a large area of land surrounded mostly by water. Saudi Arabia is in the southwestern part of the continent of Asia.

dialects (DY-uh-lekts) Dialects are different forms of the same language. In Saudi Arabia, people speak different dialects of Arabic.

Gulf War (GUHLF WOR) In 1991, the United States, Saudi Arabia, and other nations forced the Iraqi army out of Kuwait. This brief conflict is known as the Gulf War.

Islam (IS-lahm) Islam is a religion based on the teachings of the prophet Muhammad. People who believe in Islam are called Muslims.

monarchy (MON-ar-kee) A monarchy is a nation that is ruled by a king or queen. Saudi Arabia is a monarchy.

Muslims (MUHS-lihms) Followers of the Islamic religion are called Muslims. Most Saudis are Muslims.

nomads (NO-madz) Nomads are people who move around as the seasons change, living off the plants and animals around them. Some nomads live in Saudi Arabia.

oasis (oh-AY-sis) An oasis is an area in the desert that has water. An oasis is green with trees and plants.

plain (PLANE) A plain is flat, often treeless land. In Saudi Arabia, there is a plain along the Red Sea.

31

Further Information

Read It

Beardwood, Mary. *The Children's Encyclopedia of Arabia.* London: Stacey International Publishers, 2002.

Cane, Graeme, and Dynise Balcavage. *Welcome to Saudi Arabia.* Milwaukee, WI: Gareth Stevens, 2002.

Senker, Cath. *Saudi Arabia.* London: Franklin Watts, 2006.

Look It Up

Visit our Web page for lots of links about Saudi Arabia:
http://www.childsworld.com/links

Note to Parents, Teachers, and Librarians: We routinely verify our Web links to make sure they are safe, active sites—so encourage your readers to check them out!

Index